SELECTED POEMS

Also by Grevel Lindop

Fools' Paradise
Tourists
A Prismatic Toy

A Literary Guide to the Lake District
The Opium-Eater: A Life of Thomas de Quincey
The Path and the Palace: Reflections on the Nature of Poetry

Selected Poems of Thomas Chatterton [Editor]

GREVEL LINDOP

SELECTED POEMS

CARCANET

First published in 2000 by
Carcanet Press Limited
4th Floor, Conavon Court
12-16 Blackfriars Street
Manchester M3 5BQ

A CIP catalogue record for this book
is available from the British Library
ISBN 1 85754 465 X

The publisher acknowledges financial assistance
from the Arts Council of England

Funded by THE ARTS COUNCIL OF ENGLAND

Set in 10pt Garamond Simoncini by Bryan Williamson, Frome
Printed and bound in England by SRP Ltd, Exeter

For Michael,
in friendship

These poems have been selected from five previous collections: *Against the Sea* (1969); *Fools' Paradise* (1977); *Tourists* (1987); *Moon's Palette* (1988); and *A Prismatic Toy* (1991). *Moon's Palette* was published by Words Press; all the other volumes by Carcanet.

Contents

I

Ovid in Exile

At the outposts of a broken language
I have lived lately. These barbaric provinces:
the worst wine in the empire, no books, and the most
execrable climate. (I have a few notes of
such grammar as persists here, having to instruct
my servants. His Imperial Highness would not
be interested.) A poem will not suffice
for this bone-grasping cold, let alone
death, or loneliness. Like the provincials,
such things would need physical violence
to make them intelligible. The grunts
of these oxen express them more accurately.

As for you, Julia, if you expect a poem,
you can go to the Emperor and let him
fondle you with his greasy hexameters.

More real than any poem I can make
are the dreams of you that shake me
nightly, and wring me dry, body and mind.

And these I cannot send you, my dearest.

The Barrel-Dance

For a year I lived over a pub.
Monday and Wednesday mornings
I worked with half a mind, my ear
attuned to the traffic's rumblings
in the street, awaiting the warm beat
of an engine idling below:
the brewery wagon. When it came,
the world opened and I was at the window
to watch the new barrels unloaded –
not your spry aluminium kegs
but all the dead weight of iron hoop and wood

stave, and about nine gallons of beer:
a weight that if one of them took
a sudden drop could crush a man's foot
and crack the paving-stone under it.

The driver would climb up over
the tailboard, sing out for the landlord
and then with a roll and a toss
spring the first barrel over the side
of the wagon and down to his mate
who'd catch it as it fell
with a thud that shook the building
on a coconut-fibre pad at his feet
and spinning the cask on one rim
skate it towards the cellar
like a weightless dancing-partner
and juggle it horizontal to roll down the chute.

I thought no dancer or acrobat
could match the rhythm of their work,
their art of weight and movement,
but like all performing artists
they improved the world not a jot:
I never drank in the pub,
for the landlord remained a churl
and the beer in his glasses warm and flat.

Caption

Photograph of a corner-shop, its rust-red
paintwork framing a collage of gaudy
adverts, *Brooke Bond Tea, Senior*
Service Satisfy, Tizer, Park Drive
on the windows, and the interior beyond
cool blue-green like an aquarium.
A hoop-backed upright chair on the paving-stones
recalls the old woman who sat like a doll
there one hot day, eyes closed to the light,

thin wrists composed on knees, completing
my picture, I thought, until I returned
with a camera and she was gone,
just the chair keeping its spindly shadow
at the edge of the stone doorstep.
   Park Street or Albert Street, one of the places
you couldn't find now under the rubble
of demolition and the cleared earth even
with a map, any more than now
I could trace to some junk-shop that cheap
wooden chair which waits in the photograph,
stage-left, the seat still cool in the sun, for someone
who in a moment will step again
into the street and rest there.

The Tattooist

She asked me for a butterfly
there, on her shoulder. No one knows
what goes on under the skin.
I was a man with time to kill
for money, and an art to sell,
patient enough with my line
to take the minimum of pain
filling a chosen space
and never choosing the design.

I worked at a square inch,
a needle nuzzling the skin.
I wiped the blood off where the line
was drawn, a blue embroidery
in the margin of her world.
She paid, and I am free to stay
like the icecream man and the clairvoyante
and the others who sell their addictions,
and she goes wrapped in the new web of her body:
she will never be naked again.

Buying Valentines

Months can surprise us: today,
for instance, cold February holds
so many aces in her hand:
the shops blush and billow with hearts,

vermilion, cherry and lavender hearts,
all colours of the candy-spectrum –
even a few in lace. A chorus
of little whores, singing of how

you can earn love, or buy, it will be like this:
a calendarful of lipstick kisses,
sweet hearts that open for your inspection,
a mere date making a new mistress.

And February always brings them:
these paper hearts will perish, perish
and yet come back yearly like leaves
unfolding in their short season

and we buy them, thinking it's a year
since last we bought such innocence,
glad no one will open them unwillingly
unlike letters or telegrams,
or other cards the months deal out.

The Hands

Busy and blindfold, taught their trade by trial
and touch, they are naturals, eager exponents
of every half-formed thought, or of no thought.
Getting bored, they twiddle their thumbs or tap,
thinking that you are thinking nothing,
waiting to run an errand to pen or pocket.

The devil, we say, finds work for idle hands.
Idle heads will dream their own contraptions
but wreak no havoc till hands are called to service:
hands in hatred of hands hammered iron
nails into the palms, twisted a crown,
offered the dice their chance to make decision.

The pride of heads denies them understanding
then reaches out a hand to prove the world,
explain its music and articulate
precise intelligence of love. The dark,
the silent, all comply to the hand's order,
make their confession to the fingertips

as honest as those bluntly-put enquiries.
No artists, they'll create by mere assuming
as they assume you now, love, substance you
out of the night's negations. Magic of touch,
you're there again. I feel you reach towards me.
The darkness round us sings the praise of hands.

Mirror and Candle

The mirror and the candle throw
their incantation through the room
and on the wall our shadows loom
monstrous in their reverberate glow.

Their occult transformations make
our bed a range of hills, the floor
a flickering plain edged with the shore
that borders on a glassy lake.

We act our legends in that space.
The mirror takes, the candle gives,
and light from both the eye receives
to conjure out that double place

where through the sky our shadows pass
drowned in the depths that wait below.
I rest my cheek on the pillow
and in the fathoms of the glass

you reach across the dark to me.
The light flows back the way it came.
High on its tower of wax the flame
sings songs of mutability.

Bluebeard's Wife

Like Alice, I stepped into a cool mirror
to a place where the clock had a smiling face,
to a garden of talking flowers:
but when I walked the paths to meet you
began the game of hide and seek and
further you withdrew at every step
(O master of the primal mansion), further,
to tower over the trembling land
like a mirage of God on the sky, and all the while
a bunch of keys sang 'Bluebeard' in your hand,

'Bluebeard', they whispered, and the more I loved,
more I was drawn into the dark of eyes'
fathomless pupils, drowning,
swimming down until something was solid inside.
Like a small fish I curled at night
warm on a pulsing pillow,
dreaming in the red chambers of a heart,
the soft walls soothing as they surged apart

and closed again. I was a child exploring:
rooms opened into rooms, and in my hand
the keys sang at each door and charmed the lock;
rooms of the throat, the skin, the womb
unfolded, offered themselves to me,
and still I was alone until the last

door opened and I found you small and face
to face, staring at me as at a glass.
I touched you, but you didn't notice.
Now I shall leave the house and set you free.

The Spot-Welder's Song

My hand is a fist of metal,
distended limb of a cripple, slung
to the ceiling on chains and cables:
I grip the seam of this scarred hulk
in a clench like a steel finger and thumb
and the volts thud into the skirts
of this car-shell, jolt my steel clench
(its bloodless digits) numb.

My fingers are lost in their gauntlets,
my face asbestos, a cyclops-eye of mica.
I can touch nothing, nor see with a naked eye:
only the metal is naked, that spreads
under the hands I shift, and takes
each blow and burning into itself like love
or purgatory, calmly,
so it can move out scarlet or clean green
slick as a mirror in every cellulosed limb
sealed of the scars from my ham-fisted forge.

And down the chain-striped halls
components go by like hunks of meat on hooks
chained too. That insect-progress carries them
and soothes the circuits of the brain
until the hands climb their own course,
swing up the welding-gun again
(the hinge and river know it all)
grip to a seam and in my arc
fire more blind power from its source.

And you, wired harem bride for the iron Pharaoh,
new model for the sad man's lust,
love for you, if there is love, 'll be
somewhere else:
we hammer you because we must,
flat-heart machine, frog-faced queen,
hungry rust.

Ampersand

'And *per se* and', the grammarians,
the stammering pedants, christened you at first,
but at your usual short-cut game
you slipped a syllable, old escapist,
to come out like a clown with a clown's name.

I remember you in black on primrose,
twenty-seventh in my Edwardian alphabet book,
drawn as a snake tied in a knot with a grin
on its face, which pleased me more than the innocent
B-for-Baker or S-for-Sailorman.

I find you like a trickster in other guises:
rampant in gold on book-jackets as
a back-to-front 3 with a foot in the air;
or scrawled like a plus-sign by people who
don't know what you're called and don't care;

but that's all right. You'll cross any frontier
in Europe. Convenience will see you through.
Typeface jester, strange hunchback,
camp-follower of the alphabet,
our laziness & haste curl up in you.

Dictionary

Weighing perhaps ten pounds, it makes the desk
an altar. Other books and casual objects
congregate themselves around it.

It is a god: I can place anything,
whether a grand piano or a microscope
beside it, sure without checking

that inside those black covers it is named.
I can perform no action which this oracle
cannot define and number

and ratify by quoted precedent.
I imagine the books on my shelves feeling humbled:
it swallowed them all before they existed,

its belly contains infinite others like them.
Only by gibberish could they escape,
and scarcely then: it defines *Jabberwock*,

and *gobbledeygook* (substantive, US slang)
and knows who coined the words, which it takes as tribute.
It is alpha and omega.

Where shall we go to escape the eye of the god
which is Word? Into our dreams, perhaps,
the love and confusion we can't express,

for if we say them the book will swallow them
as (and here I feel a certain frustration)
it has already swallowed this poem,

motionless and emotionless as God.
I struggle to breathe parts of it into life.
The dumb, idiot book says nothing.

The Core

Cut through an apple, and you find a star.
There is a mathematics of design
and symbol in the artifice of nature:
the fall that shook the fruit from Newton's tree
pulls down the meteor, and for a sign
the apple keeps its hidden signature,
an asterisk embedded in the heart
referring to a single symmetry
beyond the laws that cut the world apart.

Shropshire Union Canal

This unexpected night,
warmer by five degrees,
cleared the coal-heaps of white,
thawed out the iced-up quays

and unobtrusively
without a jolt or shock
set the canal-boats free
and opened every lock.

II

To Scheherazade

Your unperturbed voice
with a serenely repeated movement
like the scimitar-stroke
of a great bird's wing, lays open
a rift of clear air
through our silence, a coloured swathe
engrossed with human action:
debate, betrayal, ruse, justice.

Through the page as through a pane
we look out on a spacious real world
where people say 'But Allah alone is wise . . .'
finding a baboon an artist in calligraphy
or the lost ring in the belly of a fish.

In that saying, the imperturbable
perspective: they are real
to themselves in the same way
as to us. In that, and the knowledge
(on which especially your love is founded)
that there is a story opening
inside every other story,
and that of these it is given us to know
an infinite number, but still less than all.

Monuments

I

Perfect curve, shaped like nothing
but itself. Love-object, disquieting muse:
little paraboloid moon
pored like skin, freckled lightly
at the south pole, sheened
ceramic. Cold to touch as stone. Something
rolled in sleep; weighty
in the hand. Pink tear-plummet from eye
of soft rock god. Friendly face
all gaze, no feature. Inside, messy life.

II

The sky blue tortoiseshell.
Mixed on its palette the curded marquetries
and stones, the scumbled
rag and piled muscle, a slow
pondering manoeuvre
on the estuary. Fingernail flecks,
apricot-vanilla scoop
stealing a march; the fibreglass
escarpment pitched
on a silent thunder of frozen surf.

III

Flame of deepening shadow, flexible
razor. Flat smokeplume
flaring from tapered, curvate spine; airstream
grafted to slick, horny rod. Lightshot,
silkwatered, these elastic
shreds so easily peeled
apart, as easily drawn
into an unflawed blade. A little
fluff at the base, then the clean blunt
shaft, translucent, durable and light as a proverb.

IV

Creased like a soft leather
with folding – those grained, wispy trackways
crossing a rose plain etched like a banknote
to Maori swirl of lines.
Blue cords knit and webbed under
taut, plied surface. Five branches
curl, cantilevered from central pad;
on one, askew, a gold quoit, alien metal
in this soft island. Open, meaning something –
direction, offer, welcome. A riddle, closed.

V

Sheer urgency in one direction, still
and to the point. Swordfry. Midflight arrow
secreting a drop of space
like a tear in its eye, its tiny noose, emptyface
under a bright hood, thirled
by the compacted thread. Spine
of steeltree, polished slipway
for light, cherishing fineness
towards a touchable
end that tempts, hurts like an unlit flame.

VI

Answer. Solution. Secret. Brass
gollywog. Soft notched saw.
Tarnished bar bitten
across its grooves to a mountain-range
profile of broken teeth, indentures
binding to a remote
partner of cryptic inner ways, coded
along that metal graph
like a brief song in notation, a flourish
followed by tumblers, the obedient tongue.

VII

Magic painting-book:
on a wet-ink sky
light's watercolours come clear, a hoop
of soft neons, green
the most prominent. There are no ends –
where the buildings start it simply
isn't, nothing moves and now it
wastes into air, the grey-pearl cloudbanks
or the mind's eye, an afterimage
that fades in the fixing.

VIII

Out of that tarblack pigtail pours a peacock-
blue curve up into soft
flirting spire. Lightdipped brushtip
juggling a dimmer, hazed loop in its tongue, lapping
stirred air over its shed, glassy
pool. Crisis on a tower.
The crater's lip holding, holding until
(Rapunzel!) a clear plait sinews
down, bulges, sets
to a fine rib on the ivory wall.

IX

Furled labyrinth of stained
pages, veined and deckled watercolour
or fine ink, alluring spiral to crumpled
infinities of implication, book
reconstituted from dimensions
beyond us: you compel
apostrophe and reverence. I drink you
deep in a whole breath and you're untouched:
ragged and flawless,
you promise and contain everything and have no inside.

X

Through a film of dust the finger
draws a clear furrow of bright nothing.
Those metallic specks and blemishes:
sunspots on a slice of vertigo
I pass from hand to hand. Ceiling
at the bottom of a well
flat on the table, light's
skating-rink, perception's
uneasy joke. Bending gingerly
towards me, the not-quite-unfamiliar face.

The Traveller at Yazd

He steps down from the bus
onto dust radiant with spilled oil –
the trance of journey snapped.

Round him, through him, people talk, shout,
an intricate layered trellis of noise.
Luggage is chivvied from the cargo-lockers.

The signs ahead are scarlet Arabic:
a manic exuberant scrawl
like a line of flame on the horizon.

He shoulders his pack. His footsoles
tug into the ground. The street glitters with twilight.
Nobody knows him. This is what he came for.

White Horse

1940: a summer of mythical heat,
and up on the Berkshire Downs my father in khaki
with an OCTU contingent spread out over the hillside
spading slabs of turf from the back of a lorry

to bury the White Horse. Square by square
the turf is laid and the blinding chalk goes under
the rough green skin of the down, secure
from the moon's betrayal and the jealous bomber.

When landmarks were allowed again, someone else
dug it up: perhaps he would have liked a share
in that restorative work, but had no chance
to turn his hand to it. And how much more

of England, of us, stayed buried after
those years, those wars? Whatever is concealed
may be forgotten – the moment of doubt, the toy soldier,
the gold collar sunk in the stubborn field.

Protecting ourselves, it's ourselves we bury
and with time the ploughshares of habit go over
until the desire or the thing unspoken seem ordinary
dullness lodged in stony ground. Father,

let us uncover the white horse of love,
delicate as a bone brooch, solid as the chalk
heart of the down, the ground on which we move,
undiminished, cut free and living into the rock.

My Grandmother's Opal

Nowadays I can find no picture of her.
I lost the only photograph I had
moving house; nothing else came to me,
so all I keep now is this opulent bead,

milky violet, craggy sugar-white
and crumpled goldleaf fused into the one
hurtfully alluring crystal depth
of opal, her favourite stone,

which like a scrying-globe entraps the eye;
though I should need more than a jeweller's glass
to see what figures might flaw the blue mist
or walk unscathed out of that golden furnace,

distant and enigmatic, bright and small
as now my memories of her: some stories
and nonsense-rhymes she riddled me out of her childhood,
odd scents she used, her sharp, affectionate gaze,

skirts I buried my face in, and the love
which like an animal I could discern,
inhabit like warmth but never comprehend
or, so young I was, return.

So here it is, my grandmother's opal,
centrepiece of a necklace broken and strewn
who now knows where? And of no use to me,
too large for a ring, too splendid to cut down,

message I can't read, riches not mine
to spend or give, unexplained trust I hold.
I keep it: but where shall I set it, this one spark
saved from the fiery heart of a lost world?

The Chinese Temple in Hollywood Road, Hong Kong

The dark, the dust. And then the brassy lamps
and red silk banners, muffled voices, flare
of melting candles, and the clack of lots.

Around the shrines, wreckage of joss-stick stubs
as if a colony of birds nested
in the rafters, scattering singed pink twigs,

though only the vast yellow incense-coils
spiral into the shadows overhead,
loading the air with their slow self-consuming.

A bell clangs and an old man hurries past
floundering into a black-and-scarlet robe:
some ritual business waits among the gods,

the sage with domed forehead, the bushy-browed
yellow king or the fishermen's goddess,
Tin Hao, who rides a silver fish like a surfboard.

Somewhere inside this darkness an alchemy
no one can name or bother to point out
recedes into the gloom, undisturbed.

We never touched it. At the same pace go
the colony, the hoarded pieties,
long life, good fortune, wealth, the ancestors –

rotund, bearded, smiling like Chinese Falstaffs,
they fade into the shadows; perhaps
most truly the gods as we forget about them.

The Legacy: Emmer Green, 1956

Let the boy try. The chisel's edge is slid
into the crack. A few businesslike knocks
should do it. Gently now. The blistered lid
resists, resists. He levers at the box,

I hold it steady. (All day long they've worked
to sort Miss Mary's things. A magpie-nest
of clothes, toys, jewellery, papers, bills, that lurked
in bags, chests, cupboards, clocks; and with the rest,

I'm told, the poet's letters, stuffed in absurd
odd corners. They asked *us* to have a go
at these old trunks and crates. Why she left word
the Scouts should open this, I'll never know.)

A splintering crack. It gives. A musty cover
of cloth, and under it the dull green
nubbed bulk of a fully-loaded revolver.
Army issue. Nineteen-seventeen.

Thirty corroded live rounds in a pouch
of mouldy leather. Gasping, the lads crowd in.
Treasure-trove! No. No: better not touch.
Steadying my hands, I pack the things again.

In mildewed lint and sour buttery tarnish
the huge unwieldy ghost of war is laid.
My fingers nearly slip on the dull varnish.
Lifting the box, I learn that I'm afraid.

The Suppliants

Poorer than the snail,
they hump no house on back but come
to beg though they don't know it, forming
no intention, drawn by aura of tealeaf
maybe, or spilled drop of milk
flavouring the air that threads
the crack at corner of my kitchen door.

Little-finger-sized,
two slugs without a thing to recommend them,
mere trust is all they have. They don't know I'm here
though they may feel the kitchen light
blink on or darkness plunge if I stand over them.
They don't ask for what they take,
nor could they reproach me if I killed them –

which I'd be ashamed
to do. I even wish them well,
whatever well for them may be. By dawn
they'll be gone; and if I put them out at night
they don't come back, their habits cryptic
as the tracks they leave, which answer to the moon
like veins of bright metal in the stone doorstep.

Russet Apples

Lie back against the pillows:
and again, as if for the first time,
I give you a russet apple.

In our country the custom
is love first, and then apples:
a ritual celebration
of our unhoped-for return
after aeons of wandering where
there was nobody, or the next best thing –

some lover who didn't care
enough to let it be right;
some man who wouldn't trust,
some woman who didn't dare;
where always she was hiding a hate,
or he had to fondle an image
to help him get it on.

Now we've passed the gate,
the land is ours again
and the apple's into the secret;
feel how it loves us as you bite
and the juice comes, cider-sweet,
leaf-sour, and the rusty bronze skin
gleams wet in candle-light,

and feel when I kiss you how
within the mouth's dark space
there is no I or you
but only a fragrance of endless
orchards that waited here, always
ripening, longing to welcome us
back into paradise.

Fidelities

I

A house with a friendly ghost:
he planted columbines in the garden
when he was tenant. After he died
a neighbour saw him look out of the window.
And a child's skeleton
three hundred years old
folded in one of the walls. Maybe the dead
can bear witness. We don't know.
Only it seems something is offered here
out of the long past. We accept it.

II

Tides of meadow lap the garden:
sheep jump the wall
to rip off rosebuds, tender growth-tips
of spinach, lettuce, broadbean.
Moor End Fell is a swell of woodland
to the sky, quilted
with cottongrass, oak, hazel.
The woman who welcomes us here
brings us, with the grace
and also the formality
of a priestess, food: meat, a bowl
of strawberries; homemade Martini.
'Marriage' is a word I savour,

tasting it slowly. So is 'husband'.
That sounds like a farmer. The first
like a kind of fruit.
A strawberry? Something in season.
'Wife' is firmer, like bread.

III

You drowse behind me on the bed.
Still looped in your heartglow
I sprawl in the window-seat
and read the Arabian Nights,
watching
down the smooth green
trough of the dale
last sun behind Kilnsey Crag:
where a bony elbow of rock
juts through the worn jersey
of bracken, grass, topsoil –
honest for once.
From the sky's deepening blue-green solution
stars crystallise out.

IV

We come over the top
and the next valley tilts towards us
a veined cup of stone and grass,
the far side glassy with distance,
the village caught like grit
at the bottom.
                    These friable stone houses;
and a blind white horse on the green
noses its way darkling
among thistles, ryegrass, bubbles of dandelion –
lipping the great circle of its tether.

V

Ravaged with ivy,
a secretive inn
where the kegs stand on the floor behind the bar;
the landlord circles tables with an enamel jug,
his ear atilt
to the TV set on the counter
where England are winning the Test at Headingley
on Botham's innings. Indifferent
to cricket, we breathe the excitement,
sharing a ritual
with the few customers. They let us be included, who
enjoy their elation, then our own.
As the match ends
there is laughter, scraping of chairs,
assessment of play. Nothing
shakes an essential silence
founded deeper than the stone flags under our feet.
From the wall opposite
sepia faces gaze out:
a rabbit-shoot. Lined up
for the photographer, they stand
at attention: expressionless, moustached,
twenty men
holding up countless rabbits
in rows, strung together
by the ears, like long furry
garlands looped
from hand to hand;
their own monument, not
asking for our approval.

VI

A buffeting wind:
at closing time
we find the road carries us
at once away from all that, fronting
the hillside, to cross a yard
(the ragged

timeless barking of farmdogs)
and take the bridleway
along the slope's edge
until the village drops back into the pocket
of the fell,
and we climb up into a path that leads
through the eye of a stile chipped from the stone skyline
and on like a thread
into the rest of our days.

Signal

Like a faint sonar in the night
I read your signal now, a light
Quick quiver come and gone within
The echoing depth under the skin
When my love guides my fingers to
The depth where she has sounded you.
Heavy between the tides of sleep
We wait, and feel again the deep
Disturbance gathering to break
The surface of our lives and shake
A world of habits to the strange
Designs of unpredicted change.
  Now in your secret chemical garden
Bones crystallise and muscles harden,
Directions of the will begin
To try the walls that wrap you in
And turn about below the heart
To which you beat a counterpart.
Small Jonah in the lovely whale,
You will forget to tell your tale:
What led you to these human shores,
What other name and form were yours,
What storms of fear and longing drove
Towards the little bait of love
We scattered in pure ignorance,
Caught in our senseless lovers' trance.

And now we turn again to sleep,
Under the film of dreams I keep
A sense of your live touch, that lifts
Towards us, empty-handed, gifts
Of pain and transformation, our new
Selves as strange to us as you.

Little Girl on the Lawn

She is afraid of the grass
and sits alone without moving, her
right foot held delicately,
awkwardly, up out of reach
of those rippling green tongues.

Perhaps there is too much space:
the sky is enormous blue,
the snakeskin towers of lupin
rocket into the air
their strident pinks and purples

and under the glare of sun
her mother and I are calling
out on the shimmering green
ocean where she fears
to be lost; and so she cries

and keeps her small right foot
aloft still as an amulet,
uncommitted, her own, and will not
let it step into the world
in which we have long since drowned.

Leaf Wading

For the first time she can walk
Under October trees
And feel the leaves with a soft strange shock
Crowd like a wave to her knees.

Reaching the end of the drift
She stands and considers, then
Turns back with an urge of sudden delight
To trudge through it again,

And this rare afternoon
In the brittle gold sun
Invents for herself what all children
Always have done.

Harvest

Harvest passes these suburbs without a sign
Except the apples, cheaper in the shops;
But when I lift some flagstones a harvestman
Swings out from a crevice between two slabs –
Body brown and plump as a barleycorn –
And goes with lurching gait over the concrete,
No spider, but himself a walking web,
Feeling his way with all eight legs at once.

Twilight mellows towards dusk, then hovers
Over what's visible. The stones resonate
Mildly to some light after the sun's.
I bed the last slab, straighten up to dust,
Gingerly, sand and soil from buzzing hands
And face to face meet a harvest moon
Floating remarkable over the trees,
Sharp as a blade, ripe as an apricot.

Harvestman, harvest moon – the words are blown
Here on a drift of language like husks
From seed long scattered. Walking back to the house,
I think of harvesters who worked those nights:
The swaying reaper three-legg'd with his scythe,
Binder and gleaner wakeful with the threat
Of rain, forearmed against impending winter,
Taking these extra hours of the moon's bounty –

Wading thighdeep among the silver grain
All those strange centuries before the streets
And patterned gardens were laid out like flags –
Cloud of lupin, gaudy slash of willowherb,
Laburnum powdering the usual pavement –
Their sweet pall drawn over these temperate fields
Where corn once grew, as it may grow again.

In Quintum Novembris

Summer has come to this:
a gambler's funeral.
Though you walk on wet gold
it is only that the trees have thrown in their hand,
the wind will sweep the board.
The spendthrift god lies cold.

His children have begged for pennies:
sulphur, saltpetre, charred wood
scent the approaching dark.
The sun toils in the mines of Scorpio.
Rockets assail an empty sky
and, flickering, fall back.

Dark

This is the first house where I've liked the dark.
Once night was void where backward things might lurk:
a burnt-out bulb or faulty switch meant fear,
lack of willed light the prelude to nightmare.

Not now. Closing curtains against the moon
I'm amused by how darkness closes in
reminding my hands of distance between doors,
my feet of soft carpets and counted stairs.

Is it that all ghosts have been stripped away
with the old paint and paper? Or that in me
some hidden hate has cooled and ceased to rebel?
I rejoice in the change but cannot tell.

I and the house are one. We settle down,
welcome rainfall and woodcreak. Let the night run,
let the mind's eye whose pleasure is to keep
dark in the dark mirror dreamless sleep.

Latoun

Latoun, as Chaucer called it, this fine alloy –
tin, copper, zinc and perhaps silver
hammered out to thin sheets, marked
by dint of the iron hammerhead with mottles
like the moon's face or the armour of a fish.
No lexicographer or chemist knows
how it was made, or how its name was made –
which they spell *latten, laton* or otherwise –
discarded like a fragment of old tin
which I here polish and hold up to the full moon,
its answering talisman, just naming the colour:
not silver, pale gold, mother-of-pearl. Latoun.

On White Moss

in memory of Pete Laver (1947-83)

I climb the path again,
wet clay and mud into air
sweet with must of blackberries and sodden
bracken the year lays down
as I would lay what brings me here –
question, aesthetic, love, or fear
of what might be forgotten,
or of too much remembering –
into the making of another year.

A summit grows ahead,
and then another on its back
but there's no highest point
among the shattered cubes of rock,
wet peat and heather where the tracks are lost,
all shape an accident
of weather, time, the light
cutting memory at a certain angle,
a few words from a broken conversation.

Torn edge of cloud like blotting-paper soaks
colour from the skyline. North,
the roofs and smoke of Grasmere
are huddling in, faceless
for winter. Under my left hand,
south beyond the gulf of trees,
Rydal Water like a dropped
glass jigsaw-piece glints at the sky. I stand
against a hesitant, persistent wind.

What happened to our confidence
that meaning underlay all this,
or was all this? While we walked here we talked
of Ruskin and his peacock-feather,
and of the cave Coleridge found
below Nab Scar: you planned
to follow all the hints he left
in some notebook, trace back his steps
and reach that fable underneath the ground

no one now will touch. But there you are,
hunched shoulders, toes kicking the stones,
your frown
searching the horizon for the next
sharpedged distinction or joke,
or swinging on a dead branch till it cracks
and we can drag it down, snagging and
thudding, through the trees,
then break it up to feed the cottage fire.

Only imagination loves the past
or warms its hands at those dry branches
now, so many days
of smoke have blown across
already. Passing your house
today, I found the iron gate
shut on your view of Silver How:
sweet smoke hung in the air,
someone else's cat strolled out and stared.

Everyone's a stranger. In the end
we live in one another's
thoughts: and though you move
again, I think, somewhere in the maze
of being, I can only
read you here, written into the book
of the landscape: which perhaps
is how you wanted it. When we last met
you told me of the time you walked up here

in spring, in morning, looking down
those rocks, and glimpsed a bright flutter like fire
caught in a crevice: wild azalea,
seeded from someone's garden. And I thought
of coming back another spring
to find it. Now October
wears out, and the trees
with their too-literal mourning
wait for the wind to tear their colours down.

It's time to go. Nothing's complete, a life
breaks down to fragments, the high
or low places of being. Children grow,
poems are read or forgotten,
whatever we gave someone takes.
I take your footholds down, seeing
a tract of sky that clears, rock-fragments shining
in the wet light; and one azalea,
burning and burning as the stars come out.

On Helm Crag

Height, expressed only in scraps of sound
carried up from the valley: a dog barks,
a motorcycle scores an inch of road
silence resumes; and once a child's shout
cutting thinly across the air
engraves its diamond-scratch on the clear lens
of height, through which all things appear
small and perfect, and myself invisible,
merged an instant into crag and valley
as if I too expected whatever they wait for
to happen the moment I am gone from here.

Mappa Mundi

The thirteenth-century world-map in Hereford Cathedral

for Neil Colyer

Shaped like a spread cloak, as Strabo
would have said, or for us like an envelope
with the flap up, this trimmed squareyard
of sheepskin nailed to its wooden stretcher
is space for a round world of ragged
continents, ocean-rimmed, mermaid-hymned, spoked
with a cross of seas, pivoting like a wheel
on Jerusalem, nave of creation.

Here are Babel and Rome,
the Strait of Gibraltar and the Earthly Paradise
on its island out at the sun's East Gate
with a wall of fire to deter trespassers
like us; Ararat, where in clear weather the Ark
may be seen by the sharpeyed, timbers firmly stove
on the first mountain-tip given up
by the Flood; the cannibal Essedones, and here
dogheaded Lapps, the crocodile and centaur.

Here is a mirror, and the world inside it
no stranger than your eyes, the palm
of your hand or your stressed heart bound
by its rivers of blood, home of boredom and madness,
the journey in the body's battered coracle
towards the imagined garden. Think kindly,
then, of Richard the Clerk, who dared place
his own Clee Hill in this corner, not so far
from Jerusalem but a man might hope to walk there
once in a lifetime, covering the earth
with no finer vellum than the soles of pilgrim feet.

O.S. Sheet 117: Chester

Spreading it, I uncrease a map of childhood
Sundays: Peckforton Hills' huddle of greenwood
From which the Castle jutted like a toy fort,
Suiting its name; Farndon, where I caught
Eels that thrashed on the grass to inextricable
Furious snarls of fishing-line, seamless muscle,
Red clay and tangy slime that stuck to my fingers –
Odourless now, and tracing Dee's meanders
Through pale fretwork of villages on squared paper,
The land ruled flat and stretched as compromise
Through memory's declivities and spires.
  Kinnerton, where my father's fathers farmed;
The Parks with its hayfields, where one sunwarmed
Afternoon between wars my father was photographed,

Boy in a school cap, perched on the iron seat
Of a horsedrawn reaper, where fields are reaped still,
Though nearer Wrexham now. And Bickerton Hill
To the north, where it seemed the sun always shone
So hot the hazels, sand, bracken-fronds
Glowed like copper in the wavy air
And I imagined the sun dug himself in there
At nights like a fiery hedgehog under the drifts
Of brown oakleaves and gnarled, furry fernroots,
Below the scorched hill making his restless bed.
   Places I may dream of when I'm dead,
Though glimpsed just long enough to wake the blood
With tremor of things hardly understood.
Above them, Beeston Castle on its outcrop
Of battered sandstone and, shown on no map,
The caves beneath, whose globed chambers, scooped
As if with a spoon from the honey-coloured rock,
Led from cavern to cavern, colder and further
Into the hill, where I ventured with my brother
On the damp sand floor to find the end, almost
Until daylight from the cave mouth was lost –
Almost – but could not quite bear to break
That last frail thread of light, would turn and race back
To the opening, and then again trek inwards,
Fronting the unmapped depth, hearing our shouts
Echo down into the darkness, where
We longed to follow them and wouldn't dare.

Migraine

   It begins with a cursor,
twinkling flaw in the magic glass of
   vision, a ghost-mote twirling
just off-limits: where you look it still
isn't, but now there's a tease, that haunts
   the confident panning of
your gaze, a dropped stitch threatening the whole

edgeless fabric with dissolution
and it spreads, a no-coloured shining
   seepage, irrational as
a spill of non-Euclidean space
fusing the middle of whatever
you look at: in the road you cross it's
a hole, lively as mirage over
   hot tar (negotiate this
with circumspection, out of it a
car may leap); in the book you read it's
a vibrating black-and-white flamepatch
eating the print – as if into a
pool of tears the next word you want keeps
   weeping itself until you
give up, lie back under a strobing
tornado of zigzags that simmers
down at last to a single chord of
pain, the head ringing drily to a
violin-bow of ache that floats there
like a chainsaw floating through a log.
   No one can tell what it means
or why it has chosen you. You might
suspect the boiling god of a blocked
inspiration, or guilt over some
archetypal lie; but cheese late at
night, or too much Tia Maria,
seem just as likely. The contingent
demons of physiology spare
   no one at last; they have no
art; and if this glimpse of the world in
   their distorting lens shows how
brittle our bright arrangements are, with
   that painful wisdom they have,
certainly, done for us all they can.

Summer Pudding

for Carole Reeves

Begin with half a pound of raspberries
picked from the deep end of your sloping garden, where the birds
play hopscotch in the draggled fruitnets; add
a quarter of redcurrants; gently seethe in orange juice
for six or seven minutes with some sugar,
giving the pan a ritual shake from time to time, inducing
a marriage of those fine, compatible
tastes; and leave to cool. An open kitchen door invites
whatever breeze will help itself to flavour,
attenuating it downhill across your neighbours' gardens
(be generous!) so summer will surprise them,
an unidentifiable recalled fulfilment haunting
the giant bellflower and the scarlet runners.
Now introduce your strawberries, sliced to let the pallid heartsflesh
transfuse its juice into the mass, transmute
cooled fruit to liquid crystal while you line your bowl with bread
and add the mixture – keeping back some juice –
lid it with bread, cover and weight it, chill it if you like
(as if the winter took a hand) and hoard it,
opus magnum ripening its secret, edible,
inviolable time. And when you dare
slide your knife round its socket to uncling – a sudden suck –
this gelid Silbury mined with the wealth
of archetypal summer, let it be on one of three
occasions: for a kitchenful of children
whose mouths grow purpleringed and flecked with whipped cream as
they dig
and lose, entranced, the treasure of the minute;
or for the friends around your polished table, when that soft
lake of mahogany reflects the faces
melting in candlelight and burgundy, rivers of talk
eddying to a stillness lost in taste
primitive as a language, clear as thought; or for whoever
will join you in your garden when the sun
carries out summer to the edge of dark, and stay to eat
there in the early chill as twilight gels
and owlhoots quiver from the gulf of darkness, where a floodlit
cathedral floats under your eyes, and still
(wreckage of smeared plates and clotted spoons piling the table)

after the lights are killed and the cathedral
vanishes like a switchedoff hologram, remain to plot
the moon's progress across the brimming air
scaled by the nightscented stocks, or with binoculars
arrest the Brownian movement of the stars.

The Key

Samuel Palmer sketched the hill
I climb to reach my house tonight:
the moon's a coin rubbed thin with use
wrapped in torn clouds, and up ahead
the wet road gleams with black and white.

The farm gate creaks, the farmdogs bark,
their cry torn upwards on the wind
and on the wind receding now
as five years' distance falls between
that night and this reluctant mind

that will not let the past be past
but haunts a place that cannot be
again, and like a ghost would peer
in at the glass to find myself.
I grope in memory for the key:

a door once shut is always shut,
the reader there by gaslight died
five years ago, and here I am.
The wind has torn the house away,
time and the rain have stepped inside.

The mind tugs at its guyrope yet,
as if that place were not secure
from all the winds of hope and loss;
as if the key would not dissolve
always before I reach that door.

III

Vignettes:

Twenty-One Poems for Wood-Engravings by Thomas Bewick

I

Out of some dream I wake to find myself
here between two blows of the sledge,
my task to break large stones to small stones
to be trodden under the horses' feet, chewed
by carriagewheels. The blackbird's curious eye
marks me when I look up. I throw myself into the stroke,
swing up again and he is still there
unmoved. The road like a river
turns its corner. When the shadows have turned
I shall eat dinner on the bank
staring at road metal,
pick, shovel and sledge.
Then hands will shape again to the helve,
smashed rock alternate
with a glimpse of the unsplintered world:
a windmill fading into the white sky,
a signpost pointing to nowhere and nowhere.

II

Wielding anger like a favourite stick
apt to the hand, this pursy driver
flogs his rawboned horse. Stupidity incarnate,
dully relishing the world's hatefulness.
Patient and poised over his wood block
Bewick has time to notice the trunk's end
scored with thud of axe, rip of saw;
the beechgrain patterned like a fingerprint;
also the wheel blocked by a stone
and a sign on the cart that says WOOD. Beyond them,
the natural destination of such moods:
gateshaped, also made of wood, the gallows.

III

A hard wind charges. We hurl into it,
galloping in a dream to bluster
flat a fieldful of Boney's arrogant French.
They surge around us, shout
and crash in the green spray of spring
the wind flings over the branches. Tom
leads with his cornet, heels
spurring his mount, muddying the scuffed letters.
Death or glory!
In the big house, fires
still crackle. Under the library window
the atlas incubates
in its folio index villages no one has heard of –
Omdurman, Passchendaele, Quatre-Bras.
Repeat their names: we cannot hear you
or wake from our time; only ride on,
distant and fictional as the famous dead.

IV

No one knows where I am.
Out at the edge of the world
I sit; I could go on walking
until home dwindled to nothing.
Already our house is small
as a penny loaf. If I turn
I see it over my shoulder. I can cover it with my thumbnail
then let it creep out: that notch
is the wicket gate; that thread
the smoke from Nancy's oven. I close one eye
and when the wind tugs
the housewall bulges
like a white bubble. Will father see
I have left the gate open? Does he know
I can go on walking for ever
until the thread from the house will snap
and we shall be free, my stick, my dog and me?
The wind rattles. Shall I turn back,
or go on and be free?

V

If all the world were paper, all the sea
ink, the magpie would be king. Meanwhile,
Pica pica, with his copperas-green
tail, black coat and bands of glossy linen,
swaggers: he's dandy, doctor, lawyer, parson,
mountebank among birds. What does he hunt –
ink, poison or cordial? Cocks his head
as the prize sails nearer. Rippling
from page to printed page, the ink pursues
that wry intentness, pen or graver darting
bird-beak-quick to trap the tempting image –
printing the streambank, hopping at the gleam
of its own craft caught in that shining bottle.

VI

Pushing through a weather of his own,
wrapped in hard luck as in a cloak,
here comes the man no one can blame
looking for work again. Will he stop at your gate?
He is preoccupied with his own story
and will tell you some of it if you ask,
though you will know him none the better for it.
He will work aptly and without enjoyment,
talk little, looking beyond you,
reserving judgement, being in the right.
When someone falls from the ladder
in the rickyard, or the bank fails
and the mortgage is foreclosed,
it will not be his fault, though just his luck,
he will say, as he leaves. He will come
when you are short-handed. You will listen
to his tale and hesitate. Possibly,
against your better judgement, will take him on,
telling yourself that what you feel is sympathy.
If you get what you deserve, do not blame him.

VII

I am John Cowie of Ovington,
late of Napier's Granadiers,
and these the hat and coat I wore
at Minden, Wilhelmsthal
and Warburg. Where no musket ball,
sabre or shell could find a way
now wind tugs through and rain drips
and ripe mould like velvet grows.
We trod those other fields
to mire, and slept head against stone,
savour of earth in our nostrils – but what
I saw there, no one shall know:
I have no restless dreams where I lie
under the snug blanket of earth;
and now the coat is more use than the man,
emptily scaring a last enemy,
half its brass buttons stolen by boys
and all the field under its arms.

VIII

I cross your path an instant
as you walk the wood, wrapped in daydream.
Do you not know me? Poised
on this shard of timber I gaze
into you. Not a muscle
or a whisker moves. We wait
here in the moment, our eyes
meeting in strangeness, while a birdcall
echoes in the spacious roof of branches.
The flick of a leaf, a spring
and I am gone, slipping
into the thickets of your memory.
We shall meet again. You walk on:
all around you the wood is alive.

IX

Midsummer rain, melting
all the eye sees to a plash of pewter:
grey metal sky, tarnished puddles,
the stoic windmill and stone post.
We give up pacing our own hoofprints, give up
cautiously lipping the mulch of dung, straw, grass-stalk,
mud. Rain goes on for ever: impossible
to look at anything else. But the nostril
tells other tales: the herby tang of clods
opening their mineral coolness; swirls
and shifts of air flavoured with damp bark
from dripping hedgebanks; spacious cold from the uplands;
a meadowful of green barley, simmering.
Endure, endure. We take what's given, content
though our bodies turn to mud statues and rain
carves and carves its ridges into our coats.

X

I meet myself again.
Once I would run this way
and pass some old man poking the grass
with a stick, his mind idling
on epitaphs. What did I hold? A kite
sometimes, or a top. But mostly
ran with a hoop. My wrist still feels the knack of it.
My eyes fell on this Latin spell
that conjured everything. A dream!
It is all exactly the same,
only we have changed places:
my fingers harden round the stick
and here is summer again, and a boy
bowling a hoop like a zero towards nothing –
his mindless joy, my memories,
the world's full circle.

XI

Shared guilt and excitement rope you
in, your circle pressing and toppling
towards a mystery:
iridescence of cockcrow
shrunk to a bundle of dirty feathers
twitching and tumbling across the ring.
All shoulders and elbows, one
bearing another down, you jostle
and gape, treading blood and spilt beer
into the mud. That dark whirlpool keeps
your eyes from the rainbow; through its ample
hoop stays clear as a promise
against the inklined sky, radiant with all
the seven colours of imagination.

XII

Waste sea, waste shore, paid for
in the chipped coin of shellfish prised,
chucked into the creel, rattling
like pebbles in tidesuck when you shake them down.
Seawind flavoured with absence,
cloud, gullcry over rock
scours you, the accustomed
watching for son and husband,
the price of the catch; a firm abrasion
of all that doesn't matter. The tide
is spilling into the land, the hard sandribs
melting and rippling. You raise a song,
every note of it earned and priceless.

XIII

Heaped with black fossil
wherries in cortège
ride the Tyne stylish as swans,
and coals leave Newcastle
to sow petrific forests
over England. The treeferns
of smoke, the thickets of chimneys
are climbing the air. Already
men have spun an iron web
across the gorge at Coalbrookdale.
A boundary stone like a graveslab
commemorates outmoded
heraldry; soon windmill and sailbarge
will look quaint as castles,
dwindling and glimmering across the fields' green table.
Into the toybox with them!
Out of the carboniferous rock
the steam engine clambers. The new age has begun.

XIV

Somewhere, ridiculously, a wrong turning;
how long have you been watching this?
Surely overhead it is still afternoon,
long sun slanting over the flowerpots,
the poplars shimmering behind the glassed frames.
Admit a repetitious fascination
in the pedantic accuracy
of the monkey interminably basting that joint;
still, it is time you were gone. Now concentrate.
Imagine yourself getting out of the chair; imagine
yourself turning round; now for the hundredth time try
to imagine your way out through the shadows behind you.

XV

Autumn is where things start.
About the equinox
a balance shifts: the unsettled land
tousled by rain and gales,
the trees shouldering off summer and the birds agitated,
everything moving. A time
for cardgames, portents,
turning over the accounts, taking
augury as the birds migrate.
Do not mistake the season's tang
for death's: even now
like some demotic emblem
dropped from the zodiac,
husband and midwife on the one horse
gallop ungainly
towards a birth, though perspectives
change at once and a whirling leaf
swallows them. Now choose
your talisman for the dark months:
that which survives the snow will rule next year.

XVI

Dish and chamber-pot:
between them the body's life
allowed for, grudgingly.
But the mind is judged
healthier in abstinence,
its diet a shaft of sunlight,
stone roof, stone walls, this chain –
though pacing out in thought
who knows what shrinking labyrinth
of grievance or fantasy?
Only history seems on his side:
somewhere impatient Reason is bursting prison gates,
her maenad throng rampaging
along the corridors.
Reason, that guileless goddess:
with ineluctable logic she advances,
every moment
halving and again halving
her distance from this door.

XVII

How easily the rich man enters the eye
of the peacock: bright, hard, reflective,
measuring a prudent distance;
bothered about his dignity, and my dog.
I blot the landscape cheerfully; wonder
who wraps himself in these unruffled lawns,
park and woodland fanned out round him, textured
with bird and poplar, the world his prospect,
secluded by the haha of money
from vulgar crowding. If I fought his battles
it was just so that such as he
need never notice such as I. Should I blame him, or myself?
If I had his wealth, would I do as he does?
I am human, therefore divided.

XVIII

Emptied by snow, the fields
grow stranger at twilight, detail
of ploughland, bracken and ditch blanked out
to a clean space you can only disturb.
The clumped sheep have their dole of hay:
now you walk back,
the loudest sounds your dog's breath
as he paddles nimbly on the drifts
and the creak of your boots,
every lift of the foot flinging a divot of snow.
From the village, hugging its light and warmth,
not a gleam nor a voice.
Even the mill quiet as a stopped clock.
You quicken your pace. Beside you
your earlier bootprints
look different already, pressing
away into the dark
like the tracks of someone else, who has not returned.

XIX

Why do we delight
in his poise – this boy
who must not falter, balanced, a
small quotidian god
between the stones and the corded box,
between Atlas and Narcissus,
who cannot rest his load
anywhere, or look too long
for his own face, surprised
between footfalls? Is it our want
of the simplicity
the moment leaves to him,
where there is only the task, single
mind and surefoot body
and on the stones no one to speak of
until the box thuds on the bank
and the arms are allowed to ache?
Or is it that watching him we see
plainly and with a kind of
joy, that for us too there is no turning back?

XX

My kayak beached on snow
a fallen moon behind me, I strike out
sure as a compass-needle for the pole.
If they should call me back
still these rare magnetic wastes
are proof against all voices.
Purchas, Hakluyt,
your books are laid aside at last.
No one recounts this journey.
Past, the tropics of fever
shaking their sick brocade;
past, too, the morass of the body.
Ahead, only glass cliffs
and snow like a pillow. Here
I leave no footprints. Never to have existed
is all I ask, the mind's mirror to stay
unclouded by the faintest breath
of memory. Friend,
you who come towards me,
take my weapons. The boat
is ready. Let it carry you to life.
When you wake you will have forgotten me.

XXI

At the far end of time's telescope,
Thomas Bewick, you come into sight
Resolved by the sharp focus of those two
Best lenses, history and imagination,
To move like one of your own vignettes
After the book is closed. Here is Cherryburn,
And you sent supperless to bed for some
Boyhood insolence or recklessness,
Lying awake and 'listing with delight' –
From the little window at your bedhead –
'The murmuring or roaring of the burn
In flood'; or watching at that same window
Morning after morning when you woke
'All the varying seasons of the year'
Transform themselves in a kaleidoscope
Of mist and rain, leafcolour and human
Occupation, the pane etched by frost somedays
Or beaded out of true by the refractory
Raindrops.
                    Here, as apprentice,
You walk the riverbank from Newcastle
Watching the town boys sliding on ice
'Smooth, almost, as a Seeing Glass'
Or in summer stop by the sides of woods

'To admire the dangling woodbine and roses
Spangled or powdered with pearly drops of dew';
And last, at your workshop in St Nicholas' Churchyard,
Under the adequate, mysterious Northern light
You peer, rapt, into the black slice
Of polished boxwood like a pool of ink
Where such a scene floats clear and steadies, while
With a repeated urging of the hand –
Palm snug against the graver's handle –
You coax it from the darkness, crystalline
With long immersion in your memory.
    You were cantankerous over money,
Held theories about Monarchy and God,
Were quick to sense an insult; and as surely
As Blake or Palmer, traced one of the heavens,
That place where by sheer clarity of detail
All things become their archetypes. You would
Grumble at how I trespass through your fields
Though leaving not a footprint nor a blade
Of all your wiry grass disturbed. A ghost,
I take my leave. This lens falls out of line,
We're back with words. The cat climbs to my knee.
Outside the window, white October sky.
Sparrows vibrate and squabble in the eaves.

IV

Games of Chance

One summer my grandfather broke his toe
tripping on the steps outside his bank
(this must have been in 1910 or so).
For weeks he sat at home to read and think

and contemplate, his bandaged foot propped up,
the view that spilled down from his third-floor window.
Some thoughtful friend lent him a telescope:
there was the whole of Liverpool below –

cranes, shipping, church spires poking from the ribbed
ploughland of terrace-housing; and just level
with his chair, sandstone-buttressed, scaffold-webbed,
the rising ramparts of the new cathedral

tended by busy ants. Turn the brass ring,
ease in the tube: pink stonework streams and floats,
the limpid circle catches two men perching
high on a half-built pinnacle, playing cards.

The game went on all afternoon. Next day
it was the same: up scaffold, play till noon,
hoist a few blocks, move some planks this or that way,
smoke, look at the paper, and play on.

What would you do? Grandfather thought he'd take
a hand, and wrote a letter to the foreman.
The games stopped. Did the players get the sack?
The story loses focus from there on.

'They never fathomed,' I remember hearing,
'how anyone could possibly have known . . .'
And how could we know that? There's always something
tempts us to push a story to conclusion

beyond the facts. Grandfather won the trick
anyhow. Was it an unfair move?
Perhaps, perhaps. I can only sit back
balancing issues too fine to resolve

at this distance, except through composition,
the skilled thumb fanning out the knaves and queens,
the bankhand's flourish. I pick up my pen.
Seventy years: a long time between turns;

but I have played the wild card, poetry,
that reliable trump I took good care to hoard
until the right moment. Now, please, may we agree
that the game is over, that I sweep the board?

Optics

i *Contact Lenses*

How many times have you dropped on one knee,
a wounded nymph, one hand
cupped at your eye, your hair blown back,
containing tears against the wind,
then staring into your palm
tensed for a moment and caught
like a crystal tear dabbed up
on a fingertip and considered
silently on the tongue,
that lens? Cleared of grit,
the eye gulps it again
and we forget it, except at night
when everything goes lazy
as the lenses are put to bed;
or when you lose one, jolted
by a baby's flung fist, a sudden false step
or a missed catch when removing it.
From there the stories begin:
the legendary boyfriend who picked one up on a beach;
that last dogged search when, after midnight,
having turned every soft bear end over end and side
over side with the pressureless delicacy
of a computer-graphics program,
I saw it shining, a pool of love and reassurance

in the desert of fluff and crumbs on the floor of the toybox;
and one we never found, that dropped
on an empty country road we scrutinized
until the quartz and granite chippings and the nubbly tar
between them seemed to pave
my retina but yielded
no blessed gleam until we walked away, leaving cars
or sheep to pulverize the lens as I suppose it lies
today, scattered like the fragments of our
perceptions, where a moment earlier
the humped green and mottled
sheets of mountains had gone weightlessly through,
blowing or silting, a fine crystal dust
under Red Bank and Silver How.

ii *Binoculars from Nevilledale Terrace*

For Gareth Reeves

Someone has cut this fuzzed chimney out of a magazine
and glued it slap across the pernickety castle
scissored from yellow newsprint. Shreds of ash
blown from a charred edge, the jackdaws tack and spin
in depths of gusty silence. That house of grey cards
is a slate roof and prodigiously above it blooms
a soft green web of tiny handstitched allotments,
two slant rows of lettuces like french knots
and the misty velour of an unreached emerald lawn, cut
by the hard mesh of a budding tree, fluffball
sparrows preening and dropping into space
just within grasp as it seems though I cannot
find my own hand or give it substance to clutch
for anything in this delusive globe of air.
Just a delusion also the pool, mirror-still
(reflecting dark trees and a small green gazebo),
which under my longing scrutiny reverts
to a triangle of dry grass where someone has stacked
higgledy-piggledy the panels of a dismantled shed.
Waving tentatively, scratching his ear,
peering thoughtfully into a dustbin,
here is a neighbour. As he climbs into his car
it seems each detail is of great significance –

the white smoke flowering from a slender chimney,
a lozenge of grass sprigged with neatly-crossed headstones
standing up in real 3-D in this realm
where secrets are so vulnerable to the weightless observer
skimming with the birds, who feels himself become
the deepest secret of all, as if invisible
through seeing too much, as if set free
by inability to touch a single thing
in the landscape though every heartbeat shakes it lightly.

iii *Kaleidoscope*

Let me pick up my father's kaleidoscope,
a triangular tube sealed in vermilion paper,
at one end a small boy's eye and at the other
french windows and a mock-orange tree, lost
as the left eye closes and the mind accepts
a soft-lit mandala of rainbow fragments

fanned open and floating like a Japanese paper
flower in a bowl of shadow. I could have lost
myself in that box of mirrors, adoring the fragments
of light poised by an order that accepts
each jolt, jar, shake as pretext for another
symmetrical unfolding; but the kaleidoscope

gets heavy, trembles, I must drop it – the fragments
of memory live in the body – I feel the kaleidoscope
pried from my fingers; the skin round my eye accepts
an odd cold pressure, its after-image. Like paper
cut-outs, green, violet, orange, ghosts of the lost
retinal rose-window drift from one wall to another

and purple themselves into blotchy darkness, lost
as I duck into sunlight by the french windows. Other
patterns unfurl and complicate: a kaleidoscope
of pink phlox, grass-clippings, wallflowers, leaf-framed fragments
of forgotten garden-corners, the pearly-paper
shiver of honesty by the hedge. One accepts

that imagination orders memory, accepts
that the mind's mirrors multiply sevenfold all the fragments
experience brings them. But in the honesty's paper
trembling I catch reflected a glimpse of the other
I was then, in a world lucent as a kaleidoscope,
richer in its permutation of known things. Lost

and happy I nuzzle the glass and wait for another
revelation. And here is my mother, whose hand accepts
my small grip while she opens the windows. A lost
sweet garden-wind surges, one swinging pane makes a kaleidoscope
where the mock-orange heaves and explodes in symmetrical fragments,
snowing until the steps are as white as paper.

No limit to the diffusion of the fragments,
the prisms of words that will break down the white of the paper;
the ghost-spectrum of mother-of-pearl, grasped-at and lost.

•

iv *The Magnifying Glass*
with the Compact *Oxford English Dictionary*

Dipped into the troughs of print
like a wire ring into bubble-mixture,
the black handle floats up
a segment of page bellied out
to the gentle camber of the lens,
serifs of headwords leaking
rainbows of chromatic aberration.

Words, those breath-bubbles:
their meniscus stretching, stretching to encompass
so little! As you bring up the lens
there is a point beyond definition
where the words start to blur and twin,
the parallax of different eyes can't be resolved,
the right word doesn't exist.

Sometimes, tired of searching,
you might give up, spend hours browsing through
supplement, corrigenda, spurious words, books quoted –
or stow the too-heavy volumes away
and lift the lens to the window,
prop up your page and idle the glass to and fro
to catch the flimsy, inverted

miniature slide of rooftop and floating cloud
the light spills meticulously
into your room. Serendipity
and the perspectives of idleness
have their place. That summer afternoon,
say, of the partial eclipse: warned
by neighbours squinting through old negatives

and the three-year-old in the alley
with her father's welding-mask –
a slotfaced helmet on two whitesocked legs –
you turned from the sun and focused it to a neat
bitten disc the size of a shirt button,
a fiery tadpole, a light comma that smoked
and burned itself into the paper.

A Month's Dreams

I was reading Proust. For a long time every night
I tried to go to bed early. Often I failed.
But the inner life is not so easily thwarted;
and as Longchenpa wrote, aren't all phenomena
like the shadows cast by a lamp, like the moon in water,
insubstantial, ungrounded, a cloud, a rainbow, a dream?

I found myself interviewing the famous poet
in his sitting-room. He showed me Tom King and Dick Turpin,
Staffordshire murderers, on a ledge over the door.
On his bookcase shone a silver cigar-cutter
shaped like a pike. I asked him if he possessed

a chipping from the Great Pyramid. 'No,' he said,
'but my grandmother does.' When I played back the tape
the loudest sound was the splashing of wine into glasses
punctuated by a small, brisk explosion
each time the poet lit a cigarette.

I gave lunch to a Buddhist monk, and had to drive him
to the station. All the roads were being dug up.
We missed the train and went to sit in the bar
where we were joined by a stranger who wished to ordain.
He questioned the monk, who gave him a tiny Buddha
of gold-coloured metal with indecipherable
script on the back and a small ring at the top
by which it was to be hung on a chain round one's neck.

I was photocopying my dead friend's poems
on a machine in my living friend's study. The intervals
between pages I spent dipping into Francis Barrett's
The Magus, or Celestial Intelligencer –
'the Times, Bonds, Offices and Conjuration of Spirits'.
'A fudge,' said my friend. 'It's supposed to be original,
but most of the contents are stolen from Robert Fludd.'

I went to collect my wife from hospital
and found she was having a baby. The delivery unit
was full, so there she was breathing and groaning
on a bed in the ward downstairs. The Sister predicted
that the child would be born with a caul
and the gift of second sight. In the event
to help the baby along they ruptured the membrane
(possibly also our chances of clairvoyance)
and the birth was normal. It was a boy. I had forgotten
my camera, mirror, sponge, almost everything. The room
glittered round me through a prismatic haze of tears.

Househusband

The baby sleeps soundlessly
overhead: she has emptied her
brief charge of irritable
hope and frustration in their medium
of scratchy tiredness, poured them
out in a small flood of crying
and now I can feel
a silent contented purring
lull down through the ceiling;
wind flutters the classical
chorusline of nappies,
their austere flutings
tinged white-gold
with the dry April light. No one
needs food yet. The fridge
hiccups and sings
in its sleep. At the end of the garden
the bare oak and budding
lilac propose their structures
against a sky white as
paper, translucent as time.

To Catrin, at Dawn

I wake at six to give you Ventolin
from the Oral Dispenser
shaped like a hypodermic without the needle.
You suck it like a teat,
gulping the sweet
syrup, greedily indifferent
to salbutamol, as to the asthma
that's had you down six times so far this year.

Just one year old,
you've spent more nights in hospitals than I.
Now you're ready to play:
I leave you toys, a drink, two quilts
inside your small stockade
and tiptoe on the stairs
as if a misplaced foot might crack
your bright unblemished dawn,
the clear smooth breathing you've achieved again.

Our curtains still exclude the blinding sun.
I sink my cheek into the cold
imagined alp
of a pillow, skiing the weightless drift
towards sleep. Irresponsible
at last: no need to watch your stomach
balloon, collapse, labouring to catch
thick granular breath . . . In my dream
you grow into a multi-coloured flower,

some prismatic toy
smiling and refracting light
effortlessly. May you attract kindness
that way, and give it back,
and may that be your beauty, as it is.
Stumbling partly
awake, I start to think maybe
my life has been too complicated.
May you find ways of breathing easily.

Hide and Seek

Udder-deep in buttercups the cows
swayed past and we stopped to admire them,
the swinging dewlaps, profound child-friendly eyes,
glistening jaws with their somnolent rhythm;

then climbed a bank littered with dogrose petals
and found the burnt-out hulk of a Ford Cortina,
a tarblack skeleton of blistered metals
in a circle of scorched grass. Venturing nearer

(paternal, protective), I peered in. Rusty springs,
some clotted wiring, paper-ash. I turned
to tell you it was safe. You weren't there. Things
lurched slightly. Suddenly there was a flat sunpatterned

surface in every direction: layers of leaf,
pieces of sky and path, that car. I called you.
Silence. Again? Silence, and no relief
in the fidgety mesh of woodland that concealed you

like a puzzle-picture. Somewhere in this drawing
a four-year-old girl is hidden. Can you find her?
Thickets, deep meadows, gravel-pits. Walking, calling,
I could see helicopters, police dragging the river.

There was a flavour I recognized. It was the taste
of nothing. Once in Turkey crossing the Sea
of Marmara the ferry slowed, reversed
and began a laborious circling. Someone told me

a child had fallen overboard, no one knew
quite how or when. We all hung over the side
scrutinizing a placid unbroken swell, the blue
idyll that had unbelievably swallowed

someone's life. That flavour was in the air
then: a blankness, an unappeasable nothing.
I tasted it again, scanning slopes of briar,
shouting, wandering back to the first clearing

where you stepped out from an elder-clump, very pleased:
'I was playing hide and seek!' What could I do
but toss you into the air and scold you, dazed
as the mind engaged with its happiness and the new

misty sunlight rippled the trees? Meaning
and goodness are natural; only a small part of me
couldn't look away yet from that ferry, churning and churning
its useless circle on an empty sea.

1985: Dreaming the Comet

A sill of worn green-painted wood,
A window open before dawn:
Barefoot in the mild air I stood
To watch above the starred horizon

A swallowtail of dusty gold
Stream upward from the comet's eye,
While in an unfamiliar, tumbled
Bed in the room behind, you lay

Until I called you and you came
And by the window took my hand.
What powers calibrate the dark
Reflector of the dreaming mind?

What fine adjustment brought us there
And let me call you from your sleep
Into my dream, to seem to share
That distant, enigmatic shape?

Green Man: Winchester Cathedral

Eyes do not notice
the hand's acknowledgement,
burnish of caressed oak
or whose face you touch
as you step down from the choir stalls.

You walk between his two masks:
brow moulded back into leaves,
eyelet-holes between the fronds,
foliate lip and beard –
a savage concentration

stares out of the wood
towards the high altar.
Barely noticed
between choir and nave
he guards our comings and goings –

a part of the mystery.
Did man fall and rise by a tree?
Over all our world
the forests are burning.
This church is founded on brushwood.

The Project for a New Linguistics

It will listen to the voice of the rose crying, to
the stone's solitary vowel.

It will be founded in the experience of the diligent
girl from whose lips fell pearls and rubies; of
her lazy sister who found herself uttering adders
and toads.

It will attend to the Tibetan sacred books whose syllables
    murmur themselves perpetually as they rest on the
    shelves wrapped in their rainbow silks.

It will have time for the child's first pun; for the
    old man's explanation of his life.

It will trace the calligraphy of swifts and note the
    pitches of their call.

It will eat the white snake.

First and last it will know one thing, that poetry is
    plain speaking.

Language of Flowers

Pink, pansy and leaf
Floated under the lamp
Perfect for that evening;
And what was it they said?
Not your choice or mine,
Going from nowhere to nowhere,
Arriving, always arriving.
This is the answer, they said,
This and again this,
Black penstrokes on the pansy's cheek
As far removed from writing
As eternity from time.
I could think of nothing else
But the flowers. I was utterly ashamed
Of all I could do or be.

Pansies

i

Grouped for the school photograph
they're uncannily alike:
nodding and denying and resuming
their windblown interested poise, each neck a craned green spring
to pinch the bow of its inksoaked silks,
indelible violet saturating the primrose-
rinsed cleanliness of its bib,
Pekinese waffle of pollen and an arched
minuscule tongue-tip lurking in deprecation,
as if at a touch of the pen the inkstain spreading
along each petal, growing
a Rorschach blot-butterfly, Psyche's purples, the way in.

ii

Open the box, turn the mirror over:
and there is such a blush of shadows,
the tigering enigma is a whole unspeakable
opening of flat dark pathways
into energies sudden and slow at the back
of being, of the mind, these are splashes
from an unquestioned pool
asleep, deeper than self, dreaming itself
into raptures and material patterned
blisses that foil and mantle
at the surface of light
drinking, drinking us as we drink them.

iii

Thoughtflowers, nightflowers,
Jacobean masquerade
crowding the hedgerow of my untidy garden,
heartshaped escutcheon and winestained hatchment,
ruffled shadowpinks, glimpses of love surprised,
flaring like headlamp dazzle

against dark velvet,
filmy and resilient in the cold winds of April,
hedge-courtiers teasing
with the flutter of their old names:
love-in-idleness, live-in-idleness,
kiss-me-at-the-garden-gate,
three-faces-under-a-hood,
cull-me-to-you.

The Welsh Poppy

Forgotten desires fulfilled
  are the best kind:
her yellow silks uncrumpled
  by the wind

out of their furred green case
  the Welsh poppy now
unplanned, unasked, displays –
  and unrelated to how

some years I scattered seed
  in a different bed,
dug in roots, scrutinized,
  but nothing happened.

Over starry leaves
  green springs unfurl
from weedlike beginnings
  in unpromising soil.

Perhaps there's hope:
  it may be, happiness –
once you have given up
  hope – will come like this.

Echoes

For S.A.

Each evening, once the children were in bed,
I'd climb the garden wall and scramble off
its damp, bouldery top into hogweed and nettles
round the end of the building; then among moths and headstones
to the porch, where I could ease the latch up, gently
swing the door open and hang back from the threshold
to watch a blue-grey slice of window ahead
for the scrap of black that suddenly flicked across,
brief as a trick of the fading light, but again
and again, becoming real though no less strange
with repetition. Stepping into the nave,
I would hear a small continuous rumpling noise
like someone shaking and shaking a soft leather glove
that refused to come right side out, until the waft
of air hit my cheek as a pipistrelle completed
its lap and circled my head before diving away
down the length of the church. I'd strain my ears for something
beyond that dull flutter: a chirp, an echo, some key-
signature to the labyrinth of harmonics
the bat must be threading, the sibilant cat's-cradle
of tremors pitched from the hammerbeam roof, the layered
darkness marbled with intersecting coils
of notes fanned from its diapason of squawks
by diffraction around the sandstone pillars, the floor
a stone pool whose reflective surface glinted
fugitive barks and cadenzas, except where I
was planted, a plume of muffling vapours, lit
by the flare of a curious moth. I could distinguish
nothing, though as I walked to the door my shoe-soles
released, I suppose, scuffed cymbal-crashes that burst
like surf up the walls, their last resonance dissolving
into the throat of the bell as I latched the door
with its figured bass of iron.
                                        Later that summer
we rented another house six miles away
down the coast, near a field where a noctule hunted at sunset,
ranging slowly across the sky – a small
black bird, it seemed, until it swooped and the frantic
flutter of wings came clear, a labour of flying

quite different from the hurtling glide of the swifts
with which sometimes it hunted. Taking a path
where corn-marigold and scabious straggled on
at the dusty margins of the wind-combed grasscrop,
I was almost afraid, the first time, of two people
inhumanly still, and watching me from the slope
at the western end of the field. I stared them out
and strode on over the clods as if I knew
where I was going and who owned the place
until I could see their rubber-glove hands, their faces
of swathed blue polythene sack. Standing beside them
to watch the bat sweep overhead, across
rags and strips of apricot cloud, I could hear,
all at once, the *pew, pep-pew* of its cry, a metallic
pizzicato twitched from the sky, and sensed
how the field with its drifts and spirals of air, its crop
of faintly seething insects, might be mapped
in a trawl of twilight echoes. Up at the gate
near the cliff-edge I turned and waved back at the house –
though I couldn't tell if you saw, the windows were merely
tiles of flame set into the grey slate wall –
a ritual I repeated each evening we stayed there.
The bat persisted too, even after the field
had been scalped and baled for silage, and the scarecrows
leant in a distant corner, their heads together
as if comparing notes, somehow attuned
to subtleties I had already missed.

Patchwork

I

Rooms in a house, leaves from a calendar:
The season-coloured squares, humped or askew
As sleep disposes or desire may stir
The wedding-present quilt that covers you,
Hint at some pattern that might just embrace
Both of us. Now I join you in the gulf
Of dark and warmth, of half-sleep and its scarce
Pictured insights, dream-coded, even self
(My love) dissolves; and what I find's a weave
Where thought, love, time, sense, lack come to the same
Rich text. Patchwork, dreamwork, can we achieve
What's promised by the heart's perpetual game –
The intricacies of the work as planned,
Pieced from whatever fragments come to hand?

II

Pieced from whatever fragments come to hand –
A bird-sown rowan clutching at the sky,
Lilac, rough grass, the new fruit trees we try
Lagging against the cold so that they stand
In straw and polythene – our garden's grand
Plan hasn't yet cohered. This year we'll try
Harder. A primrose's pale, lucid eye
Opens to February wind, where panned
Rainbeaten earth begs for some digging. Spring
Should help. Even child-punished grass revives;
Pansies, sweetpeas and random feverfew
Will scrawl their patterns in, recovering
Flowerbeds, flagstones, turf slabs drifted with leaves,
The season-coloured squares humped or askew.

III

The season-coloured squares humped or askew,
Pasture and cornfield tilt against the cloud,
Oak copse and spruce plantation standing proud
To hem a sky of slate- or china-blue;
A short steep lawn, and swallows dipping through
A gulley where the shallow stream is loud
With children's voices, shrilling as they crowd
Barefoot in stony pools . . . Echoes renew
Far off on this cool urban day: a dream,
Those happy fragments of last summer seem –
Eyed peacock butterflies shivering flowers
Of a baroque narturtium; pigeons that purr,
Musical through a warmth of lazy hours,
As sleep disposes or desire may stir.

IV

As sleep disposes or desire may stir
You close yourself into a single curve
Or stretch – a webbed heraldic spread of paw,
Translucent hooks quivering in milkwhite fur.
Your delicate and monumental nerve
Makes you at home: white pepper demascened
With ink-black, you fulfil some secret law
Of art and hospitality. We prefer
A house with a cat. Your small liberties serve
To keep surprise awake: velvet jigsaw-
Piece that fits anywhere, you've contravened
The patchwork's grid; now you burrow from view,
Just twitching, with one paw that's nicely preened,
The wedding-present quilt that covers you.

V

The wedding-present quilt that covers you
Is Hotch-potch, technically: no formula
Dictates its colour-patterning; a far
Subtler rhythm and counterpoint leads into
An art that hides itself, pleased to eschew
Cathedral Window, Clamshell, Compass Star
For the harmonics of the half-familiar,
The sprigged clashed cottons fading and made new.
Luxuriance cropped, leafscroll and flower entwine
Across the field bordering a white-flecked square
Of blue; splashed colours run but know their place
Like hopscotch; matched, apart, almost a pair,
Harlequin check and tendrilled columbine
Hint at some pattern that might just embrace.

VI

Hint at some pattern that might just embrace
The darkening fragments of a day, the dull
Ache that's a residue of hours too full
Of half-done jobs, an urge to plunge the face
Into cool water or sheer emptiness
Unreached by children's cries? I can't, the spell
Of love dissolved in sleep's too strong, the lull
Where all thought's poised. Your arms make me a space
That's timeless, non-Euclidean, maybe known
Only to lovers speechless and alone
Together. Harmonies of breath dissolve
Our rigid forms; a gentle chaos plays
Linked hearts' impulsive rhythms, softly frees
Both of us, now I join you in the gulf.

VII

Both of us, now I join you in the gulf
Between worlds, daughter, claw sleep's cobweb-film
From different sides. I rock, to break your rhythm
Of gulped breath and loud heart; you shine the width
Of dream-glazed pupils on me, a vexed sylph
Hunted through forest mazes. All this month
The moon's tugged at our dreams, August's shut warmth
Conjuring fretful goblins horsed on wasp
Or blundering beetle out of the hair's breadth
Tideshifts of sleep; wild garlic, cuckoo-pint
And honeysuckle sweetening the faint bilge-
Tang of the summer ditches. Let the dream-wolf
Unclench. Love's a cool spring to wash the depth
Of dark and warmth, of half-sleep; and it's scarce.

VIII

Of dark and warmth, of half-sleep and its scarce-
Acknowledged glimpses of sleep's threshold, tracks
Spilt and diverging in their own strange light
Embossed with niggly visions, here's a place
Perhaps to speak. Who we are waking lacks
The knowledge of its sleeping partner, drawn
On the breath's thread into the maze of night
Whose cryptic loot the morning memory bears –
A music-book, a staircase, a blue tax-
Return unfilled. And somewhere, out of sight,
Bathed in dark waters, bringing when reborn
Confused, oracular, to its daylight half
What gifts through gates of ivory or horn?
Pictured insights, dream-coded; even self.

IX

Pictured insights, dream-coded, even self-
Mirrored and rippling fantasies give way
To sun, birdsong, the magpies' raucous fray
Among the oakleaves and, waking the half-
Light by the door, a boy, who hauls himself
On to our sill to watch the sparrows play
Along the roof. The images of day
Are odder than the night's and ask more love,
You face the labyrinth with not one thread
But a whole tangle. My son climbs up to me,
Nestles into my shoulder. But sleepyhead,
We're late. Enmeshed, I hurry, snap, get angry.
Forcing the day like a wrong-side-out sleeve,
My love dissolves, and what I find's a weave.

X

My love dissolves, and what I find's a weave,
Jacquard of themes repressed one moment, up
And forcing others down the next, to leave
Only confusion and remorse; on top
No pattern, just the ends from a sheared crop
Of misplaced wants. How to love people seems
Harder than how to please oneself; to cope
With them's far messier than writing books
Or being simply alone. They get their hooks
Well into you, and tear. Then you recall
They're you, there is no solitude, writing looks
Out from their height. Without them what it all
Comes to is nothing, and poetry's a game
Where thought, love, time, sense, lack come to the same.

XI

Where thought, love, time, sense, lack come to the same
Realm of clear possibility yet lose
No bulk, edge, colour, force, the word we use
Is art. Kindled in solitude, a flame
Draws to its current clarity of aim
The whole vortex of mess, breaking to blues
That line a linen sky or interfuse
Shadows under the rose mountains to frame
A moment poised in an embroidered field
Where we stood once. Your thread sows through the sheaf
Of Ceres' hair knots of silk poppies, sealed
Right by their own random proportion. Weave
On weave, pen, needle, heart, what unrevealed
Rich text, patchwork, dreamwork can we achieve?

XII

Rich text, patchwork, dreamwork, can we achieve
An oracle that tells us what we want
To know, truths no one asks us to believe,
Numinous trusts whose fragile margins haunt

Thought and decision? The one who made this quilt
For our marriage-bed later walked out
From her own husband and her children, spilt
Something she must have gathered, and no doubt

Read in herself whatever made her leave.
The gift stays on, and so far I've divined
No want in it, except maybe to give
Others a happiness she couldn't find.

Perhaps we want the things we want too much,
Dragged by a look, a memory, a name . . .
Imagining we'll be allowed to clutch
What's promised by the heart's perpetual game.

XIII

What's promised by the heart's perpetual game?
Hunger, addiction, fear, emptiness, blame.
Completeness lies with others, or the dead:
And if they seem the happier, it's because
Their otherness leaves nothing to be said
About their discontent, which is (or was)
The same as ours. A land of lost content
Is radiant in this room, blocked by your long
Fanatical attention to the absent
Abstract and famishing better. Neither wrong
Nor right, the moment offers its unnoticed
Completeness in a breath, a stone, a hand,
While thought builds mazes round your having missed
The intricacies of the work as planned.

XIV

The intricacies of the work as planned
Allured the mind into a maze of dreams –
Lost mirror-gardens, time in fugue with art,
Love laced with language spiralling to reach
Harmonics such as moved the angelic forms
(Breathless, lamplit) to enunciate their laws,
Gracious at Duino and Thoor Ballylee:
Music for magic casements! But the sea
Recoils from those rockfast and rumoured shores,
The tide of words is racked with tedious storms,
Turbid with residues. We comb the beach,
Turn up each word and try it on the heart;
Offer the gods our harsh, tentative themes,
Pieced from whatever fragments come to hand.

XV

Pieced from whatever fragments come to hand –
As a called ghost might improvise a face
From crumpled linen, or as you might trace
The bow's note patterned out in dancing sand –
Ideas take form, rhythms and years evolve
Subjective pastorals, where we cultivate
Our rooms, our hearts, our words to celebrate
Small feasts or hurts, and harvest a resolve
To stay, or change. Autumn arrives again,
The days grow short, the lines are running out,
But nothing ends. The year will turn about
With stars or fog, while we try to sustain
Our love, our growth through selves which merely are
Rooms in a house, leaves from a calendar.

An Edale Sketchbook

JANUARY

Fallow under a quarter-moon
Vacant ploughland lets the season
Do as it likes this mild dead day.
Thin wind rakes across the clay
Muddy and pooled at the fields' edges,
Shivers the tarnished-iron thorn hedges
And fades among the papery grass
Still fluttering in wornout pastures.
   Only the sky tumbles with life:
Masses of cloud capricious move
Against the hills' dark parapets,
By turns corrode the silhouettes,
Cubes of black rock at Nether Tor
Melting to tousled rags of air,
And like a wet inkstain Cold Side
Runs at the sky's edge, lost and conjured.
Birds stay low. A kestrel hovers,

Madly flapping, slides across,
Hovers and flaps again, to scan
For movement in the powdered green
Of a sown field below him. Nothing
Takes his eye. The mesh of sowing
Displays its pale maze to the sky.
Catching the wind, he falls away.
    Preoccupied with nearer things,
Trailing the white lace of his wings,
A magpie floats with carrion grace
Stump to stump over the grass,
Content to strut and scavenge here
Among the leavings of a year.
Scavenger too, I cross the field
For what its sheltered corners yield
And find an emblem of the time
Dropped like a discarded costume:
Black wool mask with empty eyes,
A spine distributed like dice,
Gobbets of fleece strewn on the mud;
A thing acceptably dismantled.
The living sheep not far away
Rip the thin grass equably,
Pace between battered henhouses,
Ignore the hens' dishevelled fuss.
    Shoving against my face, the wind
Opens its brief book of sound:
Brawling echo of farmdogs;
Comment of rooks that twirl like flags
Around the rattling treetops; thin
Whine of gears climbing the incline
Up to Mam Nick where the road threads
The hills' rampart between the clouds.
    O January, twofaced god,
Stern guardian of the opening word,
Blank eye and empty mask between
The plangencies of line and line,
Tolerate our endeavour, take
The first note for the finished task,
The first stone for the drystone wall
Articulate along the fell,
The gathered crop for the first seed

Drilled to the slabby, polished clod
Skewed where our ploughing has defined
A threshold to the harrowed ground.
Nourish us with your emptiness,
Your generosities of space,
After the death, before the birth,
The fire shrunk to the clotted hearth.
    Tinge of coalsmoke hugs the village.
Under the porch at Grindsbrook Lodge
The tabby's mask of sepia flame
Broods on the savage rites of home,
Complacently displays the kill,
A dead mouse on the stone doorsill.
I pause: the yellow eyes keep watch.
But I shall not disturb the latch
Or go beyond my boundaries.
Withdrawn, implicit, meaning lies
At rest within particular
Arrangements of mist, stone and fur,
While noon prolongs a muddy calm
As if no other hour would come
With rain to wash away that high
Chalk thumbprint on the marbled sky
Or snow to load those blue milk-crates
Stacked lopsided at the farm gates.

AUGUST

Rainbow and millstone grit,
thunder piling into the clouds –
the incongruities of August: shaken ruff
of a black and white sheepdog panting
at the first-floor lintel
of a stone outhouse; spattered rowan
capital illuminating
thickets of green text;
pale stitchery of ashkeys,
deep lanes bedded down in honeysuckle
nettles and purple vetch.
A bridleway like a drystone wall
sunk on its side

in the ground: you walk
on the edges of the slabs
to Grindsbrook, where the Edale shales
hang above the stream
a cliff-face of brittle
leaves, charred edges
of a burnt book, tamped into drift
of flakes, chips, tending down
to grit and sand and the water
sliding over red rock.
Wind shivers the meniscus
of light: away in the tumbling
haycart of sky the billows
coalesce and the spattering starts
on your hands, blotting the rock,
staining its soft marbled endpapers of lichen;
plucking the stream to gooseflesh, melting the path.
Underfoot the bleeding of red clay; overhead
raindrift swerves and glitters,
playing fibre-optics where the mists break,
clot, release sheets of sunlight.
August turns her *camera lucida*,
the billion prisms in the raincloud
focusing a stump of rainbow over
Lose Hill. Films of shadow
chase across the fields. The stream
throws itself down the stone in a frigid rococo
of molten glass, air bubbles
racing in wobbling clusters under the fans
and ribs of its fussed vaulting.
Slower is the flow
of the rocks, their volcanic pour
stilled to a stacking of grainy
black cubes, to piles of soft pennies,
to lion-headed wrinkled
outcrops lipped and dewlapped
with a slabby gruel of lava.
Only the weather pursues this unfinished quarry,
saturating, eroding,
wearing the millstone cheeks
with the unanswerable persistence of water.
Grindsbrook closes in

to a locked cascade of boulders,
water dropping like a secret through fissures,
forgotten unless it emerge a moment
to whirl a handful of quartz pebbles
in the dicecup of a pitted slab.
Palms on the abrasive rock,
you grip to pull yourself
bodily out of the narrow cleft
of the gulley. Light and space
burst with a gust of wind
into your head. And floating
over the long hazed-green drop of the valley,
music: the perpetual, wholly-satisfied,
interminable grumbling lilt of sheep
and a cowman's half-bellow half-yodel:
'*hic – hic – hic – hic – hic – hic . . .*'
obscure traditional prosody of milking-time.
Over the streamhead, above you, one more rock,
a massive gritty fungus
or melted anvil cleft in two:
pulling up by the fingertips you gaze
over the top and into a pool
the size of a font: clear water,
your reflection a ragged black
against a translucence of sky
just rippled by wind, poised in a cup of stone.

SEPTEMBER

i

The hot sunlight is laid across a slicing cold
of air, so that however warm your skin,
your mind will not be comforted from the longer shadows
even at noon, the overfine gold of the birch leaves,
the too-limpid blue of a summer sky grown fragile,
paler at the edges, the horizons; however hot the rock-
ledge, its hollows are expecting the dew
to pool there and freeze before dawn. Summer's lease
is crumbling; stiffly the rowan proffers
its clusters of scarlet wax, stiffly the unfurled bracken

trembles against an air which will refine it
to its own silhouette, then to its own skeleton,
to gold, to rust, to black and into the earth.

ii

Two squirrels gambol in the intricate
rootcastle of the uptorn beechtree:
iron-red brooch clotted with stones,
fringed with fungal lace of roothair,
galleys and pits for their delight.
No one observes their shadowplay,
silhouette *obbligato*
cartwheel and arabesque
against the light, into the radical maze.

The river vanishes underground,
no one hears its nightsong
under the pebbly bed
dry now as a cobbled road,
the high stone wall that dammed it back,
the long iron screw that raised the sluice;
the glassy beads of sound,
ululating echo-vowels,
music warbling in a concrete throat.

iii

When a wall dies its secrets come to light.
A drystone wall lies down like a failed animal,
spilling its entrails out on the grass:
and here is the clean gritstone and limestone,
each cob black on one side like a burnt loaf.
Scratch it and under your nail
are Manchester, Huddersfield, Sheffield,
two centuries of mills
pocked and scored into the Pennines.
Why should anyone cherish that?
Walls grow clean again,
sun bleaches, frost and rain scour;
still nothing sneaks in as once the black winds did.
People die or move on, the trees
carry no black growthrings.

Only the walls remember, netting the valley
from end to end in their hidden veinwork of soot,
their dark secret as long as a wall is a wall.

iv

A girl in a loose coat, a long switch in her hand,
directing with a high call and a gesture of the stick,
training a pair of dogs: they weave across the field
like shuttles trawling invisible thread to cut out one sheep
and pen the others in a corner. Again the high call:
the dogs bound back, the sheep pour out over the field
in a scatter and run like spilt mercury together into one.

v

A mug of tea and a heaped sugar-bowl,
a chair beside the rusting Chrysler in the farmyard.
Green trodden mud; a radio in the kitchen.
From the dairy, the hum of the separator.

vi

Look at the hook on this gate:
smooth as a spoon, it lies in your hand
a heavy iron fish, gill-threaded
by frayed red nylon bailer-twine, its barbed
tongue blunt from latching into the leaf-thin
scrolled iron eye of the gatepost; and, before that,
into other eyes: for the hook is the older.

Since it left the forge
perhaps not a day has passed but some hand
has fed it with hooking, unhooking,
weighing or absently fingering,
tieing or chaining perhaps
once in ten years or twenty to a new post
or a new gate, till its patina
comes to your hand like a greeting
out of the old, imperceptibly
changing world of the metals
that tolerate the abrupt brief dream of man
crossing a field, closing a gate behind him.

A Path

There was a path through the long grass. Although it had rained
we walked dryshod where someone had cut a swathe
over the ground hummocked with graves near the church
to a small gate under the yew, that led out
to pasture where the sheep were settling themselves
in the lee of the drystone walls. Long blades of light
and longer shadows cut across the fields
and we shivered but were happy. Nothing to see,
really, except more small fields and more walls
and the Dale spreading on either side, one green slope
turning a warm gold in the last sunshine and one
already dark as a raincloud, sinking to twilight.
But we were newly married. Everything
was filled with the plenty of its own meaning.
Even the churchyard was changed as we came back:
the long grass by the gate was gone and near the church
was a man with a scythe, just visible in the twilight.
We'd walked out in his first track, and were returning
as he finished the job, the darkening air rich
with the juice of new-cut stalks, the long grass
falling in drifts and the path ahead of us widening
and widening until it was no longer a path.

The Beck

It was the boiling of white water drew me first:
a chant and turmoil in spate
under a scarlet-clustered rowan
that fluttered unceasingly, as if outside time,
vibrant and motionless at once in the beating of spray;
and the water foaming as if new-uttered that moment
from the earth's interior. Palms on the lichened rocks
(which were alive too with the presence of water)
I lowered myself into the cleft and drank
from cupped hands with a sudden
fierce thirst, as if I had never drunk

water before. And never such stunningly cold,
piercingly pure, flavourless and, it seemed,
evanescent water had I swallowed
until that instant. I would think, I promised,
of that water reciting itself without pause
here, wherever I might be, however preoccupied,
tired or bored, I would remember this,
rock, rowan and water.
But in my dream,
months later, it was a silent thread falling
from a mountainside above me, only breaking
to sound and spray when it splashed on the page of a book
which lay drenched and open under its downpour;
my task to climb the tussocked grass and rock
to reach it. I woke, lifting the unblemished pages,
and knew it was time to leave, to begin the next
ascent, unprepared as always, except for the taste
in my mouth of that water about which nothing can be said.

From a Flat City

Sometimes from the top deck of a bus
or the apogee of the Big Wheel at a fairground
you suddenly see them, like a pencil-smudge
or a brush-stroke of blue ink over the stacked
concrete blocks of the Hulme estate and the meat-pink
brick of the cavernous textile-mills at Reddish,
and say, 'the hills!' as if they were paying a rare,
auspicious visit. Not the prisoner's square
of sky is what we crave: we've that already,
a luminous, entrancing sky that hangs
its clouds above us, delicate and massive,
like a woman leaning over a sleepy lover.
It's earth we long for – earth heaped up like clouds,
drifted like smoke, smeared like approaching rain,
combed into escarpments or piled with forest.
Our imagination dwells in hills, but the plain
and the industrial haze deny them: it's

an achievement if you can make out Beeston Hill
from the eighteenth floor of the University Maths Tower.
Yet one morning, from my daughter's bedroom window,
between the shoulders of two redtiled roofs
I caught sight of a neat triangular peak
distinct from the clouds, apparently grassgrown, the sunlight
just dusting one edge. I had half a mind
(but that such accuracy is beyond me)
to take a compass-bearing, find a map,
identify the hill and one clear day
climb it with binoculars to sift
that window like a grain of glittering quartz
out of the city blur, and maybe see her
run to the glass and stare unseeing back
towards the hills she doesn't know are there.

Jets

Not even the sky is free of our graffiti:
air-currents all day long smudge and emboss
flock trails scrawled by planes over the blue
latitudes of summer. Fine crystals of ice
drawn by the billion through that high cloud-chamber
in the wake of our irritant particles of business,
haste, anxiety, longing to be elsewhere,
they leave the sky's intangible islands and cities
barred or netted with oblique lines. Beautiful
when a sinking sun touches them off, or a breeze
frets them to solvent lace, still they inscribe
our failure to leave anything unmarked, our helpless
filling-up of our own space, as we thicken the mind
with noise, with chatter, with a scratch-polish of dullness.
Or so the mind reflects, pondering its mirror
nature: and yet those fine-scarfed skeins express
tranquillity too and something vulnerable,
ephemeral, and though entirely our own, no less
assumed by nature than the pattern of Dorset fields
or the New Grange rock-incisions. Restlessness

is what we're made of, as much as breath or water:
you can read it there as another jet goes over
and the dwindling chord of its engine-music spreads
to a rolling monotone with a hint of thunder,
drawing a white thread into a haystack of clouds.

Clun Castle

How did it happen that at sunset I was there
climbing the mound as if I had woken into a dream
and it was important to push my way up the tussocky grass
towards a skyline seen only as a dark edge
rimming the fractured halves of the castle keep? Bats
reeled from the weedhung faces of the stone
to flip and orbit against the peacock-blue
depths of the air, then weld themselves back
in a trice to the crannies and outcrops of rubble.
The dressed stone of the West wall so kept the sun's light
that to the mind's ear it sang as it cooled
over the loop of river, lost in its glassy shadows and brood
of mistgathering trees, to the easy Welsh hills
fired and hummocked like clouds into the scarlet lake of sky.
And how could it be that almost from my feet
the hillside fell away, and there on the valley floor –
small enough to cover with the palm of a hand –
was a newly-reaped field, where someone had left
a few bales to lie, and in the midst a cart
with the tailboard down, half-loaded, as if
that task suspended by twilight were the most
ordinary labour in the world, as if
some equation were not poised there still between
promise and accomplishment, between an urge to follow
the sun's attenuation to its last green transparency
and a need to turn down again to the village,
between the gathering black of orchard and housetop
and the growing white molten bar of the moon?

Curtains

There are two kinds of people, someone said:
the ones who tug the curtains closed at sunset
and those who leave them wide open to night.
If so, and now that I've heard it, I'm one of that sort,
for the summer at least; though a saxe-blue offcut of sky
and a bread-coloured braiding of brickwork are all you can see
from this chair in the afternoon. But over the room
comes, as the shadows spill round, gathering form,
first a haze and then a recession, as if space
withdrew, or relinquished its depth, while the focus
of intensity shifts to somewhere else outside
and the sky starts to astonish you, its shred
of resonant china-blue (crossed by a bird,
a diving jet-black star) yielding to a remote
bell-clear royal blue and an unearthly violet
on which the lamp throws its mirage. Then the abrupt
drop into darkness, glass becoming mirror,
the room restored, a privileged interior
warm-coloured world part of me would reject
when I reach for the curtain and rather pause to inspect
my face, lightpatched, angular, shadow-eyed,
transparent to the unclaimed depth of the night.

Dreaming about Oxford

It's a city I must put on like a suit of clothes,
insinuating myself up a college staircase
like an arm snugging into the sleeve of a cashmere sweater.
And though my room isn't here it will be soon,
as soon as dinner's over. Already a throng
in gowns and dinner-jackets is pressing around me:
we're going to chapel, or lunch, and look, there's Bowra
bull-headed and stubby in his grey suit, like a sealion
barking encouragement. 'Ah, Lindop –'
But I'm out of earshot already, and deep in Blackwell's
or is it the Bodleian? Anyhow, here's an alcove
crammed with books, and the alcove is up on a gallery

that's lined with books, overlooking a bookfilled room
with passages opening out of it walled with books.
I begin to leaf through the books. Inside them are gardens,
and in the gardens are buildings and in the buildings
are gardens again with more buildings inside them
(there's no hurry, I can get back to college later,
I've passed the test and know I can stay here forever,
or at any rate for the moment). I keep going in,
through doors with stone mullions and doors with linenfold panelling
and sluggish unwieldy oaks with lumpy iron nailheads
and panelled deal with white china knobs and gardens
in *trompe l'oeil* perspective painted on seasoned elmboard
and the doors are becoming so many and so close together
I can't tell if I'm opening doors or turning pages.
But things are growing more spacious, the weight on my hands
is only the weight of the sheets, and to open my eyes
admits the morning and the fact that I've woken
for good or ill, though I far from certain which.

Trojan Voices

'Nos Troia antiqua, si vestras forte per auris
Troiae nomen iit, diversa per aequora vectos . . .'

Brute, then, taking full view of the island, and searching up the river Thames, built upon it a City; which, in remembrance of the late subverted Troy, he called Troynovant, or new Troy, now London. This done, he put his soldiers to tilling of the earth.

i *Poet*

The battles had all been won or avoided. What could we do
but hone fine blades to a redundant sharpness,
polish our shafts, score points and bullseyes –
the world our butts, firing-range and tiltyard?
Names of the great generals, mighty clogged swordsmen
of old, we recited and praised,
reviewing their strategies on the tabletop –
here a line, there an advance. When we woke up
the war had already started. But not like the old wars: the gods

were nowhere to be seen, both sides were soon
staled, we dug in and stared each other
out over the ditches; year by year soldiers
lounged and joked in pidgin across the checkpoints.
Skirmishes notched the edges of our weapons
but defined nothing except a diseased
persistence. The epic was stillborn. Now
it will be famine, epidemic or a bloody shambles
puts our pride out of its misery
much too late. How wistfully we long
for our previous art, for the connoisseur's approval
of a sword's rhetorical flourish in undivided air!

ii *Grandmother*

I would have been a flask of a rare perfume
distilled from spring evenings, the grey corners
of a dusty street where girls whisper together
once, then laugh at a stranger going by;
from the overhearing of parents' talk,
from singing and gossip and a letter,
from hours walking alone by the sea,
dawdling, digging a pebble out of sand
with one toe while the mind bathed
in another depth, inaccessible and protected;
from the unnoticed moments that have no words
to sweep them empty; from the covering quiet as children's voices recede,
from the renewal of sunlight when a memory is tasted
for the first time and known at last;
from the exactions of middle-age
which concentrated out of years just one drop of being;
from this empty mirror, these sundried herbs,
silence that turns with the wind all day long.

Drop by drop I would dispense all this
to those who might value its fragrance,
to grandchildren who would not.

Now nothing will be saved.
Let it smash, its essence evaporate,
war tread the shards into the mud;

nothing has the same meaning
as the three-year-old girl who follows
a puff of thistledown
circling
weightless like a sleepwalker
climbing air
in a corner of the yard.
If nothing else goes free let the wind take it,
carry that seed
anywhere out of this time and place.
Let it lodge in a crevice, let it take root and crack stone.

iii *Man*

Where do the Furies come from?
Each of us looks in his heart
and finds the cracks through which they might (or perhaps have already)
come. I neglected my father.
I failed to answer that letter.
I thought no one would notice: I told myself
it was not important, or that it was too big a task
for me, or that she deserved it, or that I
had a right, if there were any justice. Is our trouble now
no justice, or too much?
The Furies, anyhow, are haunting our sleep.
It would be something to meet death complete,
not drag this maimed past of selfishness and botched work.
There is no one to ask for forgiveness. The forgiveness of the Furies
is that they do not allow us any longer to lie.

iv *Cassandra*

The priests prod the ceremonious offal, thumb their thick books.
I am opened by vision,
split like a tree by lightning, by knowledge
that will not move a feather, though it melts
stone walls and shrivels passers in the street
to walking corpses, carrying their wounds
visible on their breasts or in their hands.
The head is a helmet so easily broken

and the whole face is blind except the eyes
which cannot tell the rest what they see.
People see
and go about their business
while the god's saliva is burning in my mouth,
I cannot spit it out nor can I
swallow and be content, there is nothing for it
but utterance, utterance,
to talk to walls, to stones,
to weeds in the crevices,
to people I can only imagine,
only my enemies because they would believe me.
If the Greek women hear of this, will they understand?
How I waited for the swordsman in Athene's house –
choosing to let it be here, in front of her altar,
reading the future in my own bowels?

v *Timbers*

Not since the abused dryads
were torn out of the heart of the wood
squealing at axe-blow and plane-rip
have timbers cried out like this
we nurtured our voices
in the whisper of footfall and echo
joistcreak that spoke 'home'
to the preoccupied man
cooling tick of a rafter
spoonclatter banging door
or in luck were cossetted to the surrendered shiver
of a soundboard under a string.

Shamming dead shamming dead
and now a myth has exploded out of our sleep
a blink a quiver a rush we are transformed
to mythological beasts
the pinewall a cataract of light howling upwards
into a turbulence of cloud
the oak rooftree an incandescent mantis
pitched to its knees
groaning into a sea of live tongues

the temple statues the painted
gods with their mouths wide open who had forgotten
they were the hearts of trees remember
where they were going and pour up into a thousand summers'
blinding leafage the roar
of their combined purpose

in the morning our ashes
tangle along the seashore in the wind, drop
and lap in smeared delicate eddies of foam

a black grain silting the ploughed furrows

not caring if they will be ploughed again

vi *Poet*

Burned out with the light of a sum total
amounting at last to zero, I was left
to feel my way with this framework of bones
and a fed skin through the animal world of touch,
knowing collusion of cup with lip, identity
of hand with woven cloth or hair, an ancient kingdom
I had never acknowledged and which seemed
sufficient, the body collaborating,
to follow its own strange laws for ever.

Nothing to do with me either the memories
that spread, clouded and fined above the dry unquestionable
calyx of here and now, a great immaterial spun
seedhead puffing itself as if I were growing
a second mind. Were others like this, was it
a tumour, an infection of being? At last,
to clear my head, I began. I must have cried
but every tear was a word; it was beyond me
or my hearers and I gave in. There seemed
no end to what I knew, but that the knowing
wasn't mine.
                    Already our language is scattered
like groundsel fluff on the wind, catching at thresholds,
housecorners, unweeded verges. I am singing it

in its own voice and know we are saying goodbye.
If there is a purpose I do not understand it,
or if there are gods or what is poetry.

But the hearers are loud again, they are calling
out of their hunger I can feed but not satisfy
for more than a moment. The back of the skull
opens. I turn with this blind mask
towards them. They want me
to tell them what they have seen.
Until I speak, they cannot believe their eyes.

Mantra

Everything turns away,
All things arise and fall –
The buzzard turning the hill
Through the jewelled mill of his eye,
The seashell turned to stone
In the slow tides of shale,
The larch lost in cloud,
The shepherd's call on the air.
The pirouetting hare
Patrols the high wood,
Rain polishes rock,
The stone bridge swallows the stream:
Nothing is still the same.
Where is stillness found?
All things arise and turn,
Everything falls away.

Recumbent Buddha at Polonnaruwa

A grain like marbling or like watered silk
flows without movement through the sleeping face:
rock-ripples tinged with rose and ash and milk,
known tastes of being, calmed, finding their place.

It is as though the rock itself had slept
to dream this shape, the eyelid's curve, the lip
smoother than any natural form except
maybe the moon's rim or a water-drop;

or as if we had sought a word to speak
out of our nature, suffering, changeable,
empty, and found at last simply this cheek
relaxing on clasped hands, and this half-smile

that flowers from more than a child's unblemished seeing
or a god's detachment. Massive, lightly creased,
the carved silk pillows a wholly human being
whose last breath has perhaps this moment ceased.